Discovering My World

What Do Bats Do?

by Melvin and
Gilda Berger

SCHOLASTIC INC.

New York Toronto London Auckland
Sydney Mexico City New Delhi Hong Kong

ISBN-13: 978-0-545-14481-0
ISBN-10: 0-545-14481-7

Copyright © 2009 by Melvin & Gilda Berger

All rights reserved. Published by Scholastic Inc.
SCHOLASTIC and associated logos are trademarks
and/or registered trademarks of Scholastic Inc.

12 11 10 9 8 7 6 5 4 3 2   9 10 11 12 13 14/0

Printed in the U.S.A.   23
First printing, September 2009

Photo Credits:

Cover: © Javarman / Shutterstock; Back Cover: © B. G. Thomson / Photo Researchers, Inc.; Title page: © B. G.
Thomson / Photo Researchers, Inc.; Page 3: © B. G. Thomson / Photo Researchers, Inc.; Page 4: © Arco Images GmbH
/ Alamy; Page 5: © Konrad Wothe / Minden Pictures; Page 6: © WoodyStock / Alamy; Page 7: © cbimages / Alamy;
Page 8: © Pete Oxford / Minden Pictures; Page 9: © Dr. Merlin D. Tuttle / Bat Conservation International / Photo
Researchers, Inc.; Page 10: © Joe McDonald / Corbis; Page 11: © Blickwinkel / Alamy; Page 12: © Merlin Tuttle / BCI /
Photo Researchers, Inc.; Page 13: © Stephen Dalton / Photo Researchers, Inc.; Page 14: © Jack Milchanowski / Age
Fotostock; Page 15: © Joe McDonald / Bruce Colman / Photoshot; Page 16: © Richard Du Toit / Minden Pictures

What do bats do in fall?

Many bats fly into caves.

Do bats sleep close together?

They sleep there until spring.

Other bats fly to warm places.

Do bats have
long wings?

They come home in the spring.

Can you find the bat's feet?

Bats that live in warm places stay home.

They have lots to eat all year long.

Most bats eat bugs.

What fruit is this bat eating?

Some bats eat fruit.

Some bats eat fish.

Can you find the mouse?

Some bats eat mice.

Most bats look for food at night.

What is this bat resting on?

They sleep upside down during the day.

 ## Ask Yourself

1. Does every bat sleep all winter?
2. In what season do bats come home?
3. What do bats eat?
4. Do most bats hunt at night or in daytime?
5. How do bats sleep?

You can find the answers in this book.